So You Want to Learn About

Turtles & Tortoises

Written and Photographs by
Katrina Willoughby

© Willoughby Arts 2018

Turtles and tortoises are reptiles.

They are cold blooded. This means their body temperature is similar to the air and water around them. Have you seen turtles sitting on a log in the sun to warm?

While turtles can be found on every continent except Antarctica, most are found in North America or South Asia. The state of Florida alone has 26 species of turtles. Europe only has 2 turtle species and 3 tortoise species! There are more than 45 known species of tortoises in the world.

Softshell turtles are only found in fresh water on the continents of North America, Australia, Asia and Africa. There are around 25 species.

Sea turtles are in all oceans except near the Arctic and Antarctic.

A group of turtles is called a bale.

Turtles and tortoises are best known for their shells.

Up to 60 connected bones make up the hard shell of a turtle. A turtle's ribs are part of its shell!

Turtle shells look like they are made of a bunch of pieces. These pieces are called scutes. It is easy to see the scutes on the picture of the turtle below. The material that makes up the shell is similar to your fingernails.

A turtle's shell grows with the turtle. The top layer of each scale or scute can shed to make room for the new scale to grow.

The sea turtle above has a hard shell. You can see its scutes.

A soft shell turtle doesn't have scutes. Their shell feels more like leather and is flexible. It is lighter and makes it easier to swim. There are bones under the shell, but they aren't all connected together like they are in hard shelled turtles. The shell is thick skin.

The top of the shell is called the carapace and the bottom is called the plastron. Tortoise shells are often bumpy, turtle shells tend to be smoother. On a tortoise shell there are rings caused from growth periods of the scute.

This tortoise has a very bumpy shell and growth rings can be seen on it.

Tortoise shells are heavier than turtle shells.

Tortoises live on only land while turtles spend part of their time in the water. Tortoise feet are stumpy and built to walk on land.

These tortoises have legs that look strong like tree trunks.

Turtles often have webbed feet and long claws. Each foot of both the tortoise and turtle has 5 toes. Sea turtles are the exception to this as they have no use for toes.

Above is a sea turtle with flippers for legs.

On the right is a close up of the front foot of a turtle. Notice the long pointed claws.

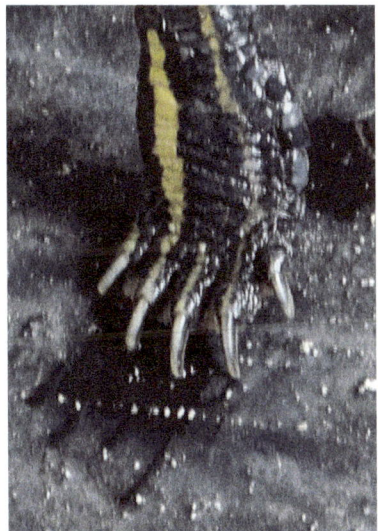

The turtles above have webbed feet with claws for use on both land and water. Their feet are different than the tortoise below which spends all its time on land.

Sea turtles can't pull their heads into their shell.

Most land turtles can pull their limbs and head into their shell for protection.

Above a turtle has hidden inside its shell from what it thinks is a predator.

Have you seen a turtle with scars on its shell?

The tough shell makes it hard for predators such as alligators to make a meal out of turtles.

Turtles are strong for their size. If a turtle gets flipped on its back it can use its strong neck muscles and head to flip back over.

This turtle's long neck not only is useful to help it get right side up, but also lets it move its head to look around.

It can hold its head high to look out of the water, or bend its head down to look where it hopes to find food.

Since a turtle is a reptile, it lays soft eggs on land. Turtles dig a hole to lay their eggs in.

The picture below shows a painted turtle digging a hole to lay her eggs in. She will carefully use her hind legs to safely position each egg.

Sea turtles leave the ocean to come on land to lay eggs. Once a sea turtle hatches, males may never come back to land and females will only come ashore to lay their eggs.

To lay their eggs, female sea turtles will return to the place that they hatched.

Turtles don't stick around to hatch their young. Some turtles may hatch when it is cold and stay in their nest till it warms up.

Whether a nest of turtles are boys or girls depends on the temperature. When it is warmer the turtles are girls!

This picture shows baby sea turtles that are being raised at a hatchery.

Turtles that live on land usually have their eyes positioned to look down. Sea turtles have their eyes closer to the top of their head. Sea turtles have glands near their eyes to get rid of excess salt from the water they drink. This can make it look like they are crying.

The picture below is a sea turtle.

A third eyelid provides a thin membrane that a turtle can see through while their eye is lubricated and protected. It is called the nictitating membrane.

Here the turtle has its eye open.

Here the 3rd eyelid can be seen covering the eye.

Turtles have been on Earth more than 210 million years. Fossils of sea turtles have been found that are this old.

The average life span for a tortoise is 80-150 years. There have been stories of tortoises over 300 years old! The oldest tortoise currently alive is named Johnathan and he is over 180 years old! The oldest known turtle was 86. Many live 20-40 years.

Pet turtles can live between 10-80 years depending on the type of turtle. Turtles like the red ear slider can live 20-30 years. Sea turtles can live up to 80 years.

This red ear slider could live to be 30 years old!

Turtles poke their heads out of the water to breathe and see what is going on above the water. Can you spot turtles as they peak out in a creek or lake? Below you can see the heads of 2 turtles and the waves they make as they swim.

Turtles breathe air and must come up to breathe if they are in water. They can hold their breath a long time. Sea turtles can hold their breath for up to 5 hours.

In winter, turtles can spend months under water. Their metabolism (need for energy) slow down so much that they can go months without coming up for air. People have seen them swimming under the ice in lakes.

When it freezes outside this turtle will bury itself in the mud under the water.

Humans breathe by using a muscle called the diaphragm to make our rib cage larger and pull air into our lungs. For the turtle, their ribcage is part of their shell so they can't move their ribs. They don't have a diaphragm. Instead turtles move their limbs and muscles around the lungs to help them breathe.

When a turtle is scared it may quickly pull its head into its shell causing air to be exhaled out quickly, making a hissing sound. Some turtles seem to have learned how to do this intentionally.

The nose on the softshell turtle looks different than that of a hard shell turtle. Instead of the pointed or rounded beak their nose may look like a horn or tube.

To the right is a softshell turtle.

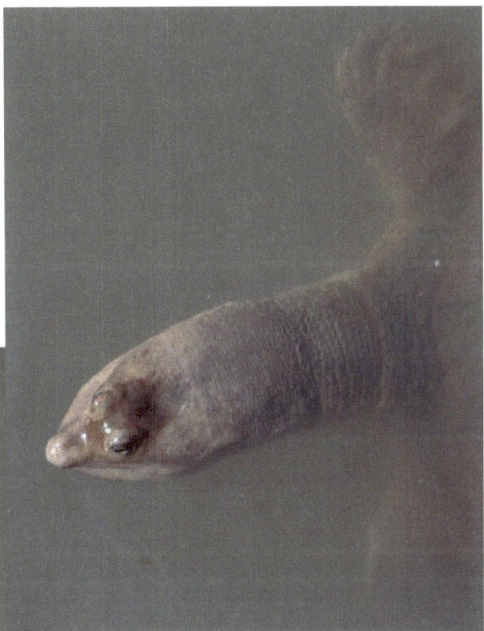

To the left is a hard shelled turtle. Can you see the difference in their noses?

Some turtles can go a long time without food. Some turtles will only eat in water. A turtle may even get food on land then take it back into the water to eat it.

Here you can see a turtle coming up from the water for a tasty snack!

Their sharp beaks are designed to cut through food. They don't have any teeth, so they have to bite off chunks that are small enough to swallow.

Tortoises are usually vegetarians while turtle
are omnivores, meaning they eat both plants
and meat.

In these pictures you
can see strong beaks on
these tortoises. You can
also see the growth
rings on their scutes.

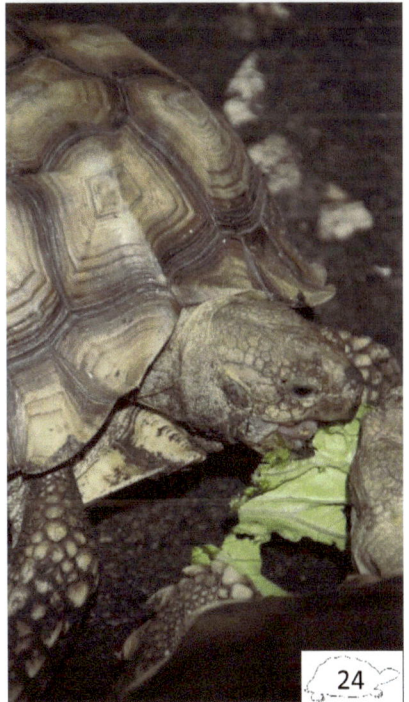

The smallest turtle is the bog turtle and its shell is only 4 inches long.

The largest sea turtle, the leatherback, can be up to 2000 lb and 6 feet long! They can even eat jelly fish.

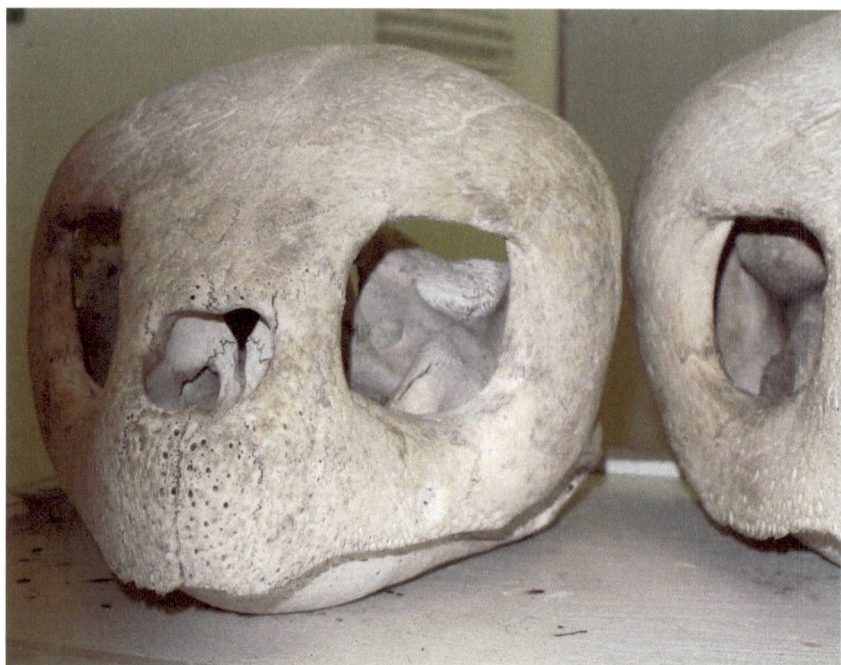

This skull is from a loggerhead sea turtle who weighed 300 pounds. Its shell was 35 inches long from the front to the back. That's almost 3 feet long!

The largest freshwater turtle is the alligator snapping turtle. It can weigh up to 200 pounds.

To catch dinner, this turtle will lay underwater and wiggle a part of its tongue that looks like a worm. When something swims in their mouth to eat the 'worm' it closes its mouth. Dinner has been trapped.

Turtles don't hear as well as people. They can't hear the high pitched sounds that we hear. A thin flap of skin over their ear bone allows the vibrations caused by sound to enter their ear canal.

Red eared sliders get their name not only from the red patches on the side of their head, but also the way they slide back into the water. Lakes and ponds may have a muddy slide where the turtles regularly get in and out of the water.

Here you can see the mud slide that has been worn into the bank from turtles getting in and out of the water.

Red eared sliders are a common pet turtle.

Have you seen them in a pet store?

Tortoises have even gone to space! In 1968 two Russian tortoises were launched to space on a rocket that orbited the moon. It landed safely back on Earth.

So….

Did you learn new things about turtles and tortoises?

I hope you learned new things and enjoyed this book!

This is the second book in the series "So You Want to Learn About…" Please check out the first book "So You Want to Learn About Butterflies" and check back for new books.

Thank you for reading.

Other books in this series

So You Want to Learn About Butterflies

So You Want to Learn About Reptiles & Amphibians

So You Want to Learn About Insects & Bugs

www.ingramcontent.com/pod-product-compliance
Lightning Source LLC
Chambersburg PA
CBHW041223270326
41933CB00001B/30